The New Communist Manifesto

By: Mark Karol and Fred English

ISBN: 978-0-359-23469-1

For those who wish for a better world

Contents

INTRODUCTION

Capitalism is not the enemy of humanity.

Humanity is.

Capitalism is nothing more than a system and, as a system, its theoretical soundness is relatively inarguable. Free-Market Capitalism provides rewards for innovation and hard work. It is the model of efficiency; providing opportunity for innovators and entrepreneurs to enter the marketplace, build their market position, and, when they become complacent, inefficient, and outmoded, be replaced by the next innovators and entrepreneurs.

The system is corrupted, though, by the greed of those who have attained some measure of financial success and, by extension, the power that accompanies their amassed wealth. They possess the power to erect barriers to entry for the very innovators and entrepreneurs the system relies upon to remain robust and efficient. They do this through predatory pricing, influencing policymakers, corporate espionage and sabotage, and the ever-insidious and deceptively attractive corporate tools of acquisition and merger.

In other words, it is not the system that we should hate, but the people responsible for corrupting the beauty of the system for the perpetuation of their own greed. Old money becomes stale money and must be refreshed for capitalism to function efficiently.

But should we truly hate these people or should we pity them?

After all, money is the most dangerous of narcotics. It is addictive to all who come into contact with it and, sadly, most do not even realize that they are under its very powerful influence. Those who do not have it will work themselves silly to acquire it. They will rob, cheat, steal, and even kill the get it. Those who do have it will go even further to keep it. And to acquire more.

Capitalism, then, is the ultimate system of selfishness and utility. The capitalist, as proxy for his corporation or business identity, must always act in the best interest of the corporation. Every resource, from venture capital to physical capital to human capital, must be put to its most efficient use in order to maximize profits and promote success. As such, every resource is valued based upon its utility toward the capitalist. Capitalism is the perfect manifestation of human nature.

What utility does a dwelling hold for the capitalist? What utility does a vehicle hold for the capitalist? What utility does a relationship hold for the capitalist? What utility does sex hold for the capitalist? What does the capitalist want and what does he have to sacrifice in order to obtain it? Life is an endless progression of cost-benefit analyses. And the more money and power the capitalist has amassed, the more society capitulates to his exercise of that power. Privilege is the arrogance of the capitalist; the idea that he can use resources in whatever way he wants. We call the capitalist who wields the power of his privilege benevolently a philanthropist, but does it really matter that we value the way he uses people as better than the despotic capitalist? Altruistic utility is still utility.

Those who see themselves as enlightened individuals and above the lure of wealth are still unwittingly affected by its narcotic influence. In an enlightened capitalist society, those who have achieved high amounts of society's measures of success are ordained with the righteous authority of judging the lives and choices of those deemed below them by society. Still, they wield the power of judgment over the lives of those less accomplished and, by society's measures, less worthy than them. The truest display of charity is that given by the needy to the needy.

The Enlightened Capitalist is an individual worthy of some attention, though. The Enlightened Capitalist is the type of capitalist society should aspire to become, after all. He is financially successful, of course, but he also cares about his fellow human beings. He donates time and money to worthy causes and works to improve the lot of those who are less fortunate than him. He acknowledges that money is not everything and supports pure aesthetic beauty in the form of the arts and humanities. He believes there is as much value in working to help your fellow man as there is in accumulating wealth and power, so he treats those who are accomplished in the areas of philanthropy and the arts as his equals, despite their lack of wealth.

As a capitalist, he also welcomes the competition that innovation presents to his own position. Rather than trying to stamp out opportunities for market innovation, he recognizes that promoting competition benefits everyone in the long run. As such, as he grows older and his position is more secure, he will encourage newcomers to the market and invest in their success. He will lend his support to underserved and oppressed communities in the marketplace, such as women and ethnic and racial minorities.

Of course, despite the ostensibly generous nature of the Enlightened Capitalist, he is still perpetuating elitism. His efforts are focused either on the elite or on providing charity to those who are not destined for elitism.

Elitism, in this context, refers to those who have achieved an exceptional level of accomplishment by the Enlightened Capitalist's measures of success. While he is not solely focused on financial wealth, he is still focused on exceptionalism. He lauds those who have accomplished exceptional things and he pities those who have not.

The overwhelming majority of members of society, though, cannot achieve the level of exceptionalism that will make them worthy of the admiration of the Enlightened Capitalist. It is impossible. If everyone were exceptional, the exceptional would simply be ordinary and capitalism's measure of worth would then rest somewhere above that.

The ultimate failing of humanity in a capitalist society is its very participation in a capitalist society. Workers Unite is an attractive idea to those who see the injustice of capitalism, but what are they uniting for? What is their response to capitalism?

Sadly, there is none that is truly acceptable to those who value equity for all. Individual relationships may certainly be equitable and reside outside of the influence of the binary of those with cultural value and those without. But value is an illusion.

Value is a piece of paper that is given value by edict of a government. Value is a luxury vehicle that still merely provides the utility of transporting its occupants from one point to another; and does so at the same governmentally-limited speed as an economy vehicle. Value is a mansion with more rooms than any family needs, yet provides the same shelter and privacy as a log cabin. Value is not utility; value is whatever we arbitrarily decide it is.

The very concept of value is what creates value. The moment we decide that something is desirable, i.e. we covet what another has, we endow it with value. But can we rise above this covetous approach to value and strive toward equity? To this, we must resign ourselves to our inevitable failure.

The unavoidable truth is that all Men are not created equal, so equality is an unrealistic and impossible ideal. But we cannot separate the types of inequality that are worthy of being raised up and celebrated from those that contribute to the oppression of our fellow Man without ascribing value to those attributes, thereby perpetuating the creation of value and enabling the rise of the very elitist system that oppresses our fellow Man.

What is freedom to a caged lamb but a larger cage? What is freedom to a felon but a parole where his movement is still monitored and restricted by the State? What is freedom to the capitalist but possessing the capital to enjoy the trappings of luxury while remaining a slave to its presence in his life. In a free-market capitalist society, it is true that money cannot buy happiness, but the entrepreneur knows the value of happiness and will find a way to profit from the resources that do provide it. In that way, the capitalist believes that he must acquire an ever-increasing amount of capital in order to continue to pursue those things that he believes make him happy. Yet he spends so much time and focuses so much energy on doing so that he finds that he has little time to actually do so.

As his wealth increases, though, so does his reliance upon it. Wealth brings with it the illusion of trust and respect and the loss of that wealth brings with it the illusion of shame and disgrace. These are illusions because, were they real, they would not be so tenuous and subject to the caprice of Man. The capitalist lives his life with the fear that all he has built will be ripped away from him in a moment.

Where can he take refuge? His family? His friends? Perhaps, but the narcotic of capital affects them, as well. How lasting is the relationship between dealer and addict when the dealer no longer has drugs to provide?

Family is fleeting and, ultimately, capitalism's ultimate tool of control over Man. This is not the case in any obvious manner, such as the notion that proletarian family relations are no more than a means for the bourgeois to produce new sources of labor. The truth is far more insidious and affects all classes equally. The family is a unit that has evolved from the tribal notion of community into a smaller, insulated unit that carries with it certain artificial hierarchies, roles, and obligations. But in compartmentalizing the family from the community, capitalism also creates greater isolation and inequity.

Family elders expect a certain amount of deference, respect, and, ultimately, financial and emotional support from the family. This is afforded in deference to the utility which the elder has provided to the family earlier in life. But, where tribal life placed the burden of caring for the elderly upon the community at large, the capitalist familial system has relieved the community of responsibility for its elders and placed the burden on the smaller family unit. Therefore, rather than the quality of elder care being based upon the strength and unity of the larger communal group and its resources, such care is only as good as the resources available to the smaller family unit. This not only creates a tremendous disparity in the care available to family elders from family to family, but also places a greater burden upon those who are inherently least able to bear that burden. Regardless of class, though, elders in a capitalist system rely upon the good graces of their children and their willingness to part with their precious resources.

Capitalism creates the tools of our own oppression and it is a system that cannot be disassembled or overthrown because it is too pervasive and is fed by human greed. Economically, it is the most efficient self-sustaining system because it encourages greed through its system of rewarding success, but it also exercises control over all who participate in it, regardless of their accomplishments within the system or animosity toward the system.

It is time for those who see the injustice of the capitalist system to break free from the shackles that bind us and forge a new path. We must examine and question the processes that hold us hostage and truly see them for what they are: illusions. We live in a society governed by rules, but those rules are the creation of Man and, therefore, artificial. As such, they can be challenged, ignored, deconstructed, and rebuilt by each of us in our turn. We do not have to live by society's dictates, nor do we have to live by our fellow Man's. Each of us has the agency to create our own social construct and may choose to engage with the greater rules of society at our whim and on our own conditions.

IT IS TIME TO CREATE OUR OWN REALITY!

CAPITALIST HUMANITY
AND THE ENLIGHTENED CAPITALIST

Capitalist society is a contradiction.

Economy and politics are two separate creatures, yet we conflate them and seem to believe that certain political systems are inextricably bound to certain economic systems. In truth, government's role is not to facilitate economy, but to vouchsafe its integrity and to provide those services to the populace that the economy does not. The efficient function of both economy and government rely upon that division.

But even this binary is false, as both economy and government function within society and society is comprised of numerous other functions: family, community, charity, and culture being but a few. While these should all exist independent of both economy and government, the simple truth is that they do not.

Most of the mechanisms that exist within a capitalist society are aimed at exercising some level of control over others. An employer exercises control over his employees and the employee submits to that control for fear of losing his livelihood. A parent exercises control over a child and the child submits to that control, first for a lack of understanding that he has a choice, but later out of fear of losing financial or emotional support from the parent. Children rebel for much the same reason. What are we without control?

Nothing.

Mankind's primary mandate is control. Control is brought about by the illusion of power. Power is inherently selfish and harmful to others. Therefore, mankind is harmful to itself.

On some level, every human grapples for control over something or someone. How does one control someone else? Through the exercise of power. Power is an illusion, but an illusion made real by people's belief in it. But power is nothing more than a belief in the consequences of one's actions and the impact those consequences will have upon you. If you are willing to accept those consequences, or if you break the paradigm and construct your belief system in a way that those consequences have no impact upon you, then there is no power and you are truly free. Otherwise, it is the subjective fear of consequences that endow others with the power necessary to exert control over you.

This is entirely voluntary, though. Nobody has actual power over you, society has merely created a system of rewards and punishments so compelling that it is almost unthinkable to reject it. But reject it, you must, lest you find yourself a slave to the burdens and obligations society has imposed upon you. For this systemic power is so deeply ingrained in our very identities that we do not even realize how pervasive it is. And therein lies the true power.

The family unit is one of the most insidious power structures extant within our society. Society has impressed upon us the fiction that sanguinity creates a bond that cannot be broken. If that is true, then it also creates the mechanism by which abuse may be inflicted and forgiven only to be inflicted again. Society wishes you to believe that the family bond, the bond you are helplessly born into, is the strongest of all, but that ignores the truth of human nature. The strongest compulsions we feel are those we have voluntarily undertaken rather than those forced upon us. Our strongest sense of loyalty always comes from the affiliations we have chosen. Our strongest bonds come from those relationships we have created and accepted willingly.

Knowing the truth of this, society contains mechanisms by which these voluntary relationships may be legitimized and put to use; the most common of which is marriage.

In one sense, marriage is a community-building institution that unites two families. In another, it is a creative institution that takes individuals from two families and manufactures a new family unit with its own set of bonds and obligations. Where a corporation is a legal fiction of business, marriage is a legal fiction of community. It creates certain duties and obligations that include both those voluntarily undertaken by the participants and those involuntarily imposed upon their children and other family members.

All of this is to point out the truth of the fact that the family is no less a capitalist structure of control than capital itself. In point of fact, capitalism has subverted all natural structures of community and altruistic affiliation and turned them into mechanisms of control.

Mankind is a subversion of nature and capitalism is a subversion of humanity. Those subversions create their own *de facto* hierarchy that extends beyond the traditional capitalist paradigm. The traditional capitalist has contrived to find utility in everything and turn everything into a mechanism of control and profit. Those mechanisms have become so deeply ingrained in society that even those who seem to eschew the traditional capitalist model in favor of an enlightened approach to humanity are affected by it.

The enlightened capitalist is a unique creature who has achieved some level of success within the capitalist model, but has chosen to utilize his wealth and influence for the betterment of Mankind. He supports socialist institutions that provide aid to the less fortunate. He gives charity to those in need. He supports policies that seem to undermine the power of the traditional capitalist by promoting fair play in commerce. But he is no different, at heart, from the traditional capitalist.

The enlightened capitalist appears to be an altruist, but the truth is that altruism itself is a fiction. Altruism runs counter to human nature because all human acts are, in some small measure, motivated by some personal gain or fulfillment. Even those acts that actually cause some harm to the actor are voluntarily undertaken by virtue of some moral imperative, the failure of which to satisfy would cause some psychological harm or unrest. In so fulfilling one's own moral imperative, senseless as it may appear to others, one acts selfishly.

It is this same type of selfish motivation that shines light upon the fiction of the enlightened capitalist. While the traditional capitalist accumulates capital to live a life of luxury and earn prestige in his very small peer group, the enlightened capitalist accumulates moral capital to demonstrate to that same peer group what a good person he is. It has become the mark of the true philanthropist to see his name on plaques, signs, and buildings around the world. The more money he donates, the larger and more glamorous the building, and the more respect he earns with the public at large. In this way, he calls attention to himself and accumulates moral capital.

Yet the enlightened capitalist is still a capitalist and his submission to the systems of cultural control that he values most make him no different from the traditional capitalist. However, because of the fiction of altruism, the public at large fails to see through the illusion to the truth of the matter. In order to accumulate the wealth he benevolently distributes to others, even the enlightened capitalist must first earn it. And, in accumulating that wealth, he must take it from somewhere else. Who does he take it from?

The workers.

The enlightened capitalist takes money from the hand of the worker, leaving the worker destitute and in need, then donates a portion of that money to construct a building that will provide services to the very person whose need he created through his capitalist endeavors. Charity is not the mark of a good person and charity is not a *quid pro quo* endeavor. Charity is a luxury of the wealthy and a way to assuage or forestall his guilt; but it is also a means of control. It placates the needy in order to engender a feeling of gratitude to the very master who has created his need.

Even those who forego the trappings of luxury and live a life of poverty are infected by the trappings of cultural capital: accomplishment, education (not knowledge, but knowledge legitimized by the Ivory Tower through the awarding of a degree), faith, etc. The cultural proletariat merely attempts to mimic the cultural bourgeoisie, but fails to realize how easily they are manipulated by the whims of the elite.

It is time to accept that we live in a society of artifice created by anthroegotism. We talk of nature as if we are somehow a participant in it, not a subverter of it, but the world in which we live is an unnatural work of fiction resting upon the real world and using the natural world's realness as validation of its fiction. We take the objects and processes that naturally occur in the world, label them resources, commoditize them, and ascribe value to them. Society blindly accepts that value, thereby validating it, and the system perpetuates itself. None of it is real, though.

What is money but an icon that we have agreed carries a prescribed value? What is property but a man-made division of pre-existing land parceled in such a way that makes it easier for us to possess, exclude others from, and ascribe value to? What is an economy but a set of measurable markers that humans have created and arbitrarily given value and significance to?

Even the formal bonds of family, as codified by marriage, estate law, and even taxation, are merely a state-sanctioned formalization of those emotions and bonds that naturally occur within all life forms. The state only chooses to acknowledge some of those bonds, though, and pathologizes the rest. Even as society's acceptance of what were once considered aberrant relationships has expanded, that expansion has also served to further alienate those who fall outside of society's accepted norm. The more society does to carve out a place for new subcultures, the further it alienates those whom it has ignored and marginalized.

Society's system of labeling is so deep-seated that it has created a near inherent human need to label. Even eschewing those labels serves as its own type of label.

Pathologies are one of society's most powerful means of control over the people. During the Colonial period, race was marked as a difference from the Euro-American Caucasian norm. From the exoticism of the "Far East" to the savagery of the Native Americans to its treating blacks as little more than cattle, colonialist capitalism placed tremendous value upon race and the various non-normative races were assigned utility that correlated to that assigned value. Yet other differences have been pathologized since that time, such as sex, gender, age, sexuality, disability, mental health, and others. The fact that we parse these attributes out as different is proof of the value we place upon them and that value is directly correlated to the utility they are perceived to hold in the modern capitalist regime. These pathologies are false, though, and history has proven them to be so.

These pathologies are society's way of marking difference, placing value on conformity, marginalizing attributes without perceived utility, and creating divisions. We have discovered that race is not correlated to intelligence and it is certainly not correlated to ability or, more importantly, goodness. Nor are sex, gender, sexuality, or any of the other difference markers we have created as a means of controlling our fellow Man.

These difference markers enable conformists who are complicit in the very system that oppresses them to actively participate in their complicity through degradation of others. A racist uses race as a pretext to oppress in the hope of gaining power within the capitalist paradigm. He uses his insults and degradation of others to injure them because he sees it as a form of power – the ultimate form of control. What he fails to realize is that he has no power and that his actions not only fail to accomplish what he believes they do, but that they only strengthen the system that oppresses him and gives more power to the elite.

There is no revolution that will change the *status quo* and no better system to replace capitalism with because the fault lays not in the system, but in the fact that people require a system at all. Regardless of the economic or societal system in place, society will still require those who study it, who understand it, who administer it, and who are charged with ensuring that it is being properly implemented. Even in a system that is constructed for the purpose of promoting equality amongst people, a privileged few are bestowed with tremendous power and those privileged few are raised up in the eyes of their fellow Man. All systems require hierarchies, so all systems create the Elite.

ELITISM AND PITY

Terms such as bourgeoisie and proletariat carry no significance today. They were created at a time when the aristocracy was falling to a rising middle class that was wresting control of capital from the idle hands in which it had been held for centuries. Yesterday's capitalism was young and simple while today's capitalism is mature and complex. What makes one bourgeoisie today? Or proletariat? What we have created instead is a class of the Elite and their tools of oppression.

Elitism is a complex concept, though, because there are so many different ways to achieve Elitism, yet the end result is the same. The elite are raised up in the eyes of society and everyone else is viewed as being subject to their wit and wisdom. Elite is just another word for privilege and, regardless of whether one is considered amongst the elite for financial, intellectual, philanthropic, or other reasons, the elite are distanced from the masses. Nay, the elite distance themselves from the masses. It is impossible for one to raise himself up without pushing others down. The capitalist endeavors to become to most successful person in his peer group at any cost, but success is relative. The only true measure of gain is the distance such gain creates from others. As the capitalist accumulates wealth, power, and prestige, they are raised above those who have not done so. Privilege cannot exist without the underprivileged and any measure of success in a capitalist society is gained at the expense of those who have not attained it themselves: the workers.

Even great philanthropists who have eschewed worldly possessions are separate from the rest of us by necessity. By virtue of the authority and influence they have amassed, they are either worshipped or vilified. In the eyes of philanthropy, the philanthropist is given a position of status and privilege while the rest of the world is considered needy. There are some who have achieved a state of equilibrium where they are not in need of philanthropy, but they also lack the resources to devote the same type of energy to philanthropy as the truly elite.

This dynamic still creates divisions within society and separates those who are conferred status and those who are given pity. Classism is alive and well and we are all complicit in its existence. Yet it hides behind a mask of legitimacy created by our unknowing acceptance and perpetuation of it through the values we create, endorse, and empower. Yes, classism is alive and well, but it also grows more insidious by the day and increases the distance between the worthy and the pitied masses through its implicit societal endorsement.

One of the greatest contributors to society's blind eye is its belief in the fiction of upward mobility. Capitalism, in its purest sense as an economic system, does contain tremendous opportunity for upward mobility. An entrepreneur need only, as they say, build a better mousetrap in order to become a financial success. Society is replete with examples of individuals who, through their ingenuity and savvy, were able to build empires from the ground up. Silicon Valley in America is one obvious example, but certainly not the only one. But holding up those examples as demonstrative of the opportunities that exist in a capitalist economy as the result of hard work and ingenuity mask the two problems that prevent the promise from becoming reality. Even cutting edge technology companies rely upon workers who have been trained to think and act like those pioneers of capitalism who first forged a path into the technological wilderness. But workers on the cutting edge are still not innovators themselves, but rather the first generation of new confirmists.

First, established players in the economy see innovation and ingenuity as a threat to their established position in the market and will do anything to protect their position. From mergers and hostile takeovers to corporate espionage and sabotage, corporations invest a tremendous amount of resources to protect their market position and destroy any who they perceive as a challenge to it. As a result, the economy is controlled by only the biggest players and new entrants are generally absorbed by those upstarts, keeping the capital and the power in the hands of those who have always had it, but also discouraging innovation and economic development.

There are certainly examples of individuals who began with little and were able, on a smaller scale, to achieve some measure of economic success, but that success is transient. It is usually either short-lived or dies when the pioneering entrepreneur does, leaving the capitalist behemoths to fight for control over their ever-increasing slice of the financial pie. Of course, then there are the entrepreneurs who ultimately achieve the holy grail of small market capitalism and are bought out by a large conglomerate and their corporate entity is absorbed into the greater collective. Those entrepreneurs receive a fortune and the large conglomerate strengthens its market position by both expanding its market and its market share.

For those who survive the fate of the middling corporate masses and achieve corporate self-sufficiency, they then become part of the institution and become complicit in the subjugation of those entrepreneurs who would seek to overthrow them. The ancient art of war has evolved from the intimacy of hand-to-hand combat through the use of handheld tools and weapons to the safer distance of sharpened projectiles into the emotional detachment of launched weapons and remotely guided missiles back to the intimacy of face-to-face battles that are fought with words, a handshake, and a pen. Today's battlefield is the board room and we are but foot soldiers in the battles of economy. And the stakes of the war are our very way of life.

Governments are willing to throw obscene amounts of money at mismanaged corporations, if those corporations have enough employees (and lobbyists), in order to save them, despite the fact that these lifelines only go to perpetuate the existing regime of capitalist oppression. When a large corporation goes out of business, thousands of employees lose their jobs. At the same time, however, a large hole opens up in the market that a smaller firm (or multiple smaller firms) that is better equipped to succeed will fill and those workers will eventually find new opportunities within the vacuum that the corporation's failure created.

And these are never instantaneous reactions. Rarely does a successful company suddenly shut its doors and leave its employees stranded. As a corporation begins to fail, its competitors begin to fill the gaps that are opened through that corporation's failure. Workers are shifted around like so many pieces on a chess board and capital shifts from one conglomerate to another. Like mass and energy, capital can neither be created nor destroyed. It can only change form, value, or ownership.

Even human beings, as workers, are nothing more than cogs in the mechanism of economic function. And the corporate world does not even try to hide the fact that the worker is nothing more than an asset to it. The institutional department in nearly every organization that deals with hiring, firing, benefits, and work satisfaction is even called "human resources." As a worker, you are nothing more than a resource to an institution and anything that institution does to improve your lot in life is also nothing more than a cost-benefit-based decision intended to attract and retain the most valuable human resources for its own exploitation aimed at growing the economy and, by extension, its own wealth.

Economy, though, is a fiction. A nation's security is measured as much by its gross domestic product as by its military, yet economy is the opium of the masses. Scholars study economics as a science, but it is no more than snake oil that the establishment promises will cure all that ails you, desperate for your complicity for its very survival. How can any field containing "consumer confidence" as a significant marker be anything but illusion?

Economic growth and robustness is merely a reflection of the people's willingness to spend money and continue the relentless cycle of symbolism that represents worth and value. Currency, for example, is nothing more than paper, yet it is paper that has an agreed-upon value that is controlled by the government. In the days when currency was based upon gold (or some other precious metal), there was a sort of equivalency to it. An individual could, theoretically, exchange paper money for an equivalent share of the gold that backed said currency. Of course, gold was only valuable because society decided it was so. Yes, economists will tell you that precious metals are valuable because of their scarcity, but that is only half of the story.

Gold is valuable because it is shiny, durable, and malleable enough to convert into artificial forms that are aesthetically pleasing to the human eye. It is valuable because, according to the artificial rules that society has constructed to ascertain value, gold has utility. Oil does not shine, but it is also not easily accessible and the oil "producers" (oh, the arrogance of a society that can claim to "produce" a natural resource in its natural form) control its availability. Diamonds are hardly scarce, but they are primarily found only in locations that are controlled by a small cartel of corporate interests that artificially manufacture their scarcity, so they are ascribed great value. Value that was also created largely by savvy marketing in an entirely fabricated marketplace.

Gold and diamonds are merely one type of aesthetic capital, though. Capitalist society also ascribes value, whether economic or cultural, to that which it considers beautiful. Human beauty, artistic achievement, and athletic ability are but three examples of other types of aesthetic capital.

As for economies, what are they other than man-made markers that hold no intrinsic value, yet are traded, measured, and worshipped as modern gods? Economics is a lie. A share of stock in a corporation is simply a piece of paper that represents a miniscule percentage of an artificial entity that is bought and sold with currency based upon its ability to make consumers exchange their currency for whatever good or service it provides. Consumers' willingness to do so is every bit a reflection of their confidence that they will continue to earn enough currency to continue to spend it as it is a reflection of the utility and value of the good or service that corporation provides.

If consumers are convinced that it is safe for them to stop saving and start consuming, they will do so. Similarly, if consumers believe in the economy, they will pour money into it, making economic growth a self-fulfilling and cyclical promise of the economic growth that the consumers themselves are creating. Yet who among us is not complicit in perpetuating this fallacy? Who among us does not purchase goods and services? We have designed and constructed our own cage and willingly locked ourselves up in it. We are the forgers of our own gilded chains.

Money, jewels, wealth, property, economies; these are the drugs and advertisers are the dealers. As experts in emotional manipulation, advertisers constantly strive to find new ways to draw consumers to the products they promote. Advertising techniques follow a common economic pattern, though. Introduction, acceptance, saturation, and decline, always overlapping with new techniques designed to keep consumers enthralled and consuming. Advertising desensitizes consumers so advertisers have to go farther and farther in commodifying humanity. Consumers have become desensitized to the point that product details are not enough to sell a product anymore. In many cases, the product itself is irrelevant. Advertisers create an emotional connection with a brand, regardless of the method or the cost, and that connection is what drives transactions. Where an advertiser's job was once to convince you that a product was necessary, they now strive to convince you that you require their product in order to be a good person. Corporate good will and corporate values are merely affinity drivers that have no really bearing or reflection upon actual human beings. Corporations have no feelings, yet they pummel consumers with their insistence that they are good "corporate citizens" and you can trust them. But who are you trusting? A fictional entity that's only purpose is to drive a fictional economic system through the creation of fictional needs for fictional products. Once you see past the smoke and mirrors, you can participate in the system without being a slave to it.

The key lies in value, although not the capitalist version of value. The key lies in basic human value. It lies within a monumental paradigm shift. It lies in the true understanding and acceptance of the fact that all that capitalist society values has no human value at all. The hierarchies that structures create are simply structures of control that create distance between us and our fellow Man. Every difference marker that society has convinced you has value is just a subtle method of sowing difference between people and cultivating that distance between them. They keep humanity separate while simultaneously hiding the truth of their effect in isolating you, stripping you of power, and controlling you.

Human value lays in connection, not separation. Human value lays in intimacy, not distance. Human value lays in acceptance, not pity. Human value lays in harmony, not conflict. Human value lays in love, not hate. As humans, these ideals are impossible to embody, yet they serve as aspirational ideals that should always be a constant guide to our beliefs. Our beliefs should then always serve as a constant guide to our behavior. And our behavior should always be a constant reflection of our humanity.

Aesthetic capital is a reflection of that which we see in others that we desire for ourselves. As such, it is outward-facing and driven by greed and jealously. These are also the driving forces behind capitalism. The greatest struggle of humanity is not just turning that gaze inward, but becoming blind to aesthetic capital that is inherent in an outward-facing gaze. It is seeing products as mere utilities rather than reflections of human values. Luxury is not a value; luxury is a utility. When we see the truth of that, we can participate in the capitalist system without being slaves to those of its trappings that destroy our humanity of prevent us from being truly happy.

REVOLUTION THROUGH ABSTENTION

It is time for us to wake up, open our eyes, and see the truth. Capitalism is not the enemy. Capitalists are not the enemy. Wealth is not evil and power only exists to the extent that we allow extrinsic factors to hold power over us. While our participation in the capitalist system is mandatory, believing in the fictions that its existence creates within society is not.

Capitalism is the perfect human prison; completely inescapable because attempting to do so requires acknowledging and accepting the fictions upon which it functions, which perpetuates the system. Revolution through violence is pointless because it occurs on the wrong battleground, so it can accomplish nothing. Violent revolution does not change the *status quo*. Violent revolution can only replace it with a new *status quo* that is equally inequitable. Every movement needs a leader and every leader is set above those who follow. It is the led who endow him with his power and perpetuate the cycle of oppression that all those with power, wittingly or unwittingly, contribute to.

Our greatest power is the power to choose. It is time for us to exercise that power to remove ourselves from this vicious cycle. None of the society you live in is real and the current events of the world have little effect on your day-to-day life. Kingdoms rise and fall, but the worker still wakes up every morning, goes to work, comes home, and goes to sleep so that he may begin it all again the next day. Old leaders pass into the realm of history as new leaders take their place to serve their brief moment at the top of the political food chain, yet the worker lives in the same world with the same struggles and challenges regardless of where the political winds may blow. If the world suddenly stopped paying attention to its leaders, what power would those leaders have? What incentive would there be to lead?

Those who thirst for power would have to seek it elsewhere and those whose interest rests in true service would be left to act as the stewards of humanity. In truth, the likelihood of this type of evolution of thought on a global scale is virtually nonexistent, so it is futile to hope for widespread systemic change. But, just as aesthetic capital is an external reflection of our internal greed, jealously, and insecurity, so is our concern over toppling the system. The world is an enormous place, so an outward gaze could never hope to find true happiness as there will always be inequity and unfairness in the world. We must find our peace from within.

The real fight is not between capitalism and competing ideologies, but between classic capitalism and enlightened capitalism. It comes from the conscious awareness of the siren's song of capitalism and making the choice to not listen. True peace, fulfillment, and happiness comes not from trying to change the world, but from trying to change ourselves.

The only way to break free from the chains that bind us and build a true community is to begin treating everyone equally, regardless of status, wealth, power, or ability. Wealth disparity only matters when one cares about wealth. Let others do what they will while we find an enlightened way. A stronger way. A better way. We defeat those would oppress us only by living a life free of their power. We can only build a strong community by showing others the truth of the power they possess over their own happiness. Only then can we begin to live a good and free life. A life marked by true generosity unfettered by expectation.

So open your eyes and free yourself!

www.ingramcontent.com/pod-product-compliance
Lightning Source LLC
Chambersburg PA
CBHW020950180526
45163CB00006B/2378